I0148919

HUNGER STUDY GUIDE

JON L. DYBDAHL AND J.D. CROFT

Energion Publications
Gonzalez, Florida
2021

ISBN: 978-1-63199-749-5
eISBN: 978-1-63199-750-1

Energion Publications
PO Box 841
Gonzalez, FL 32560

https://energion.com
pubs@energion.com

ACKNOWLEDGMENTS

When it was suggested that a study guide should be written as a follow-up to the book *Hunger*, I knew that because of my recent diagnosis of Parkinson's disease that I would need some help. God provided that help through Pastor JD Croft. Pastor Croft completed his undergraduate education at Calvin College and went on to earn a Master of Divinity degree from Princeton Theological Seminary. Because JD is also my grandson, I knew that he had a heart for God and a keen interest in theology and the spiritual life. Thankfully, JD was happy to be part of this project. His contributions were substantial and varied. I want to acknowledge his vital role and express my deep appreciation for all his time and all the ways he helped to bring this project to completion. Both JD and I would also like to thank our wives, Kathy Dybdahl and Maeghan Croft, for their input, support, and patience. Without their encouragement these pages would not have been written. Our corporate prayer is that this little book will be a blessing to all who read it.

— Jon Dybdahl

NOTE ON SONG LYRICS

The chapters in this book each include some song lyrics that connect with that chapter. When these songs are in the public domain, we have included lyrics. Where possible, we have also included links to lyrics, music, accompaniment, and/or a suitable listening track. Each link is accompanied by a QR code. If you have a smart phone, you can point your camera at the QR code and access these aids. If a song is not in the public domain, we have included links only.

Please adhere to copyright and public performance laws when using these materials in a public setting.

— The Publisher

TABLE OF CONTENTS

PREFACE/INTRODUCTION

The book *Hunger* was meant to be a Biblical introduction to the Christian spiritual life. Now it's time to dig deeper and broaden our understanding and experience. Since there are many different types of people and a variety of responses to the spiritual practices, I want to explore the avenues that help us go further in our experience of God. This little book can be used in many ways. It can be used by a small group for Bible study, or it can be used by an individual who wants to go deeper in his or her devotional time. We recommend that if you are reading this alone and not in a small group, to have a pen and journal handy, as many of the activities will ask you to write down your reflections if you are not able to share them with others. It can be read simultaneously with Hunger, chapter by chapter, or it can be read on its own after you have already read *Hunger*. You can use all of the suggestions in any given chapter, or you can pick one or two that particularly appeal to you. I am simply trying to point to the roads that can be taken as we move deeper into our relationship with God.

Each chapter will begin with an invitation for God's presence to be in and among us. We invite God's presence so that He may guide us while we try to discern His word and His will for our lives. This section will have a hymn or poem for you to reflect on to prepare your hearts. After the invitation for God's presence, there will be a section reviewing the material from the corresponding chapter of *Hunger*, along with a few related questions to catalyze thought and conversation.

After reviewing the reading, you will encounter a Biblical story that is related to the chapter and topic at hand. The stories of the Bible have a profound way of meeting us where we are and touching our lives. More and more people are realizing that stories are instrumental in our understanding of Biblical truth; Jesus was a master storyteller and almost all of His teaching was in the form of stories or parables. One of the most beautiful things about the stories of the Bible is that they have many different layers — they can be understood on a very concrete, simple level, but they can also be unpacked in a way that stimulates and puzzles even the brightest theological mind. I hope that the stories that are retold will help model what it means to dig deeper into our relationship with God.

Each story will be followed by a section dedicated to application for life. I hope to show how the stories and spiritual disciplines found in the Bible are related to us today by presenting different activities that propel us towards new growth. As was mentioned earlier, feel free to participate in as many or as few of the application activities as you wish. God approaches us all where we are, and that often looks very different for each of us. The last section of each chapter is dedicated to the works of fellow travelers. Here you can find different books and resources that will help you grow as you continue your walk with God.

This introduction wouldn't be complete without an acknowledgment of the underlying principles from which this book comes — a conviction of the grace of God and a sensing of His presence. Many of us have had a run-in or two with a particular kind of Christianity where "grace" isn't liberating or joyful. Some of us were taught that grace is something that we have to earn, and that to receive it we must dress in a certain way, say the right things, or worship with the right people. This is wrong. God is not a dictatorial figure sitting on His throne in heaven, waiting for you to make a mistake so that He might withdraw His grace from you and condemn you to hell. True Divine grace can be defined as such — God's *unmerited* favor and *His* actions on our behalf. God's grace is unmerited — there is nothing that we can do to deserve it. We will never be good enough — and that is ok, because when God looks toward our evilness, our wretchedness, our filth and our sin, He doesn't see it. Instead He sees His son, nailed to a tree, proclaiming "It is finished".

God's grace is also His action on our behalf and not our own. God has given us His divine grace, and he continues giving it to us — every second we are alive, every moment we inhale breath, with every new beginning, God proclaims over His creation — "It is good". It is out of this realization of divine grace that we can begin to invite the presence of God into our lives. I like people to deliberately open themselves to the sense of the presence of God. For many people, devotional exercises are solely a heady experience: you learn something about God, you ponder some theological notion, or you learn a fact of Scripture. One of the presuppositions of *Hunger* and this study guide is that it is good to have a devotional life that involves the inviting in and sensing of the presence of God. We want to strive to know God not only with our heads, but with our entire being, and that includes our hearts.

I had an assignment to teach a class in Christian spirituality. As I thought about how to conduct the class, I became more and more convicted that the class should take place not simply as an academic endeavor, but as a moment in time to sense the presence of God. My own life has been touched by Christian music that attempts to lead one into God's presence. What came to my mind was the song, or should I say chorus, entitled "Into my heart". From my generation, most Christians knew that song. And I thought to myself — let's try singing that at the beginning of each class with a deliberate desire to create a sense of God's presence. I began to do this on a regular basis, and several students were moved by it, and I think that the same can happen for you. Accompanying this song I would raise my hands in supplication, asking the Lord's presence to be there. The class would immediately become quiet, and together we sought to experience the presence of God and be aware of His peace. So I conclude my introduction to this study guide by inviting you, individually or as a group, to join me at the beginning of chapter one in using this song as a means of inviting in Jesus' presence and grace.

Chapter 1

Universal Hunger

Invite the Presence

If you are going to understand the word of the God you hunger after, it is important to first take the time to invite Him in — into your heart, into your mind, and into your soul. Sing, read aloud, or thoughtfully ponder the following song.

Accompaniment

Listening

- https://www.youtube.com/watch?v=gBvuxCkXXdI (Accompaniment)
- https://www.youtube.com/watch?v=t67reFUtbk0 (For Listening)

Into my heart, into my heart,
Come into my heart, Lord Jesus;
Come in today, come in to stay;
Come into my heart, Lord Jesus.

> Out of my heart, out of my heart,
> Shine out of my heart, Lord Jesus;
> Shine out today, shine out always;
> Shine out of my heart, Lord Jesus.

~ Harry Clarke

REVIEW THE READING

1. The first chapter in *Hunger* begins with my testimony of discovering my hunger for God and realizing that the hunger I felt was common among many in the church (p. 1–3). How have you experienced a deep and meaningful hunger for God? What does this hunger feel like, and what does it make you want to do?

2. The chapter continued by talking about the many different reasons that spiritual hunger is so predominant in our society today (p. 3–8). How have you seen this spiritual hunger manifest itself in the world around you? In what ways can you relate to those around you who are also spiritually hungry?

3. In this chapter, we also learned about the *double longing* and God's desire for us (p. 8–11). Take a moment to ponder the significance of the knowledge that God deeply longs for an intimate relationship with you. What emotions does this bring forth? Does this seem too emotional or touchy-feely, and why?

BIBLE STORY — PSALM 42

David is one of the most relatable figures in the scriptures because of his rags-to-riches trajectory and the numerous predicaments he always seems to find himself in. David was the youngest of eight sons born to a man named Jesse. Back then being the youngest son was the equivalent of being the runt of the litter. Property, titles, and honor were all passed down through the males in the family, from oldest to youngest. As you can guess, being the youngest of eight sons didn't bode well for David's future as a landowner and man. But God had other plans — God had chosen David to be the next King of Israel. And when God chooses someone, you know that they are going to be in for a wild ride. David fights giants, liberates cities, sneaks into enemy territory, becomes the King of Israel, and more. But it wasn't always glory and victory for David — he also experienced many hard times, often because of his own sin. David murdered people, committed adultery, and repeatedly defied the commands of God.

David wasn't perfect — he wasn't even close. But the one thing that always remained constant, both in his triumphs and in his failures, was his hunger and thirst for God. David is known as the "man after God's own heart" because he constantly pursued an intimate relationship with God. One of the most difficult times that David went through in his life was when his son Absalom rebelled and tried to kill him. David loved Absalom, but Absalom betrayed him and wanted the crown for himself. After talking to the people and winning their favor, Absalom declared himself King, causing David to go into exile in fear for his own life. David felt tremendous pain because he loved his son and didn't want anything bad to happen to him, yet here his son was trying to subvert his kingship and overthrow him. The loss of the support of the people of Israel must have confused David greatly — after all, God had appointed him King! Why was God allowing all of this to happen?

Instead of turning his back on God during this tragedy, David continually sought after Him, even when he heard no answer or reply. The Psalms give us a window into David's pursuit of God, and Psalm 42 shows us how intensely David longed after God in the midst of his own discouragement and loneliness.

> As a deer pants for flowing streams,
>   so pants my soul for you, O God.
> 2 My soul thirsts for God,

for the living God.
When shall I come and appear before God?[b]
3 My tears have been my food
    day and night,
while they say to me all the day long,
    "Where is your God?"
4 These things I remember,
    as I pour out my soul:
how I would go with the throng
    and lead them in procession to the house of God
with glad shouts and songs of praise,
    a multitude keeping festival.

5 Why are you cast down, O my soul,
    and why are you in turmoil within me?
Hope in God; for I shall again praise him,
    my salvation[c] 6 and my God.

My soul is cast down within me;
    therefore I remember you
from the land of Jordan and of Hermon,
    from Mount Mizar.
7 Deep calls to deep
    at the roar of your waterfalls;
all your breakers and your waves
    have gone over me.
8 By day the Lord commands his steadfast love,
    and at night his song is with me,
    a prayer to the God of my life.
9 I say to God, my rock:
    "Why have you forgotten me?
Why do I go mourning
    because of the oppression of the enemy?"
10 As with a deadly wound in my bones,

my adversaries taunt me,
while they say to me all the day long,
   "Where is your God?"

11 Why are you cast down, O my soul,
   and why are you in turmoil within me?
Hope in God; for I shall again praise him,
   my salvation and my God. (Psalm 42)

David craved a deep and intimate relationship with God. With his world swirling and sinking around him, David continually turned to the one with whom he was most intimate. As you embark on this journey into the spiritual disciplines, be encouraged that you are not alone in your yearning. When you are in the middle of the wilderness and your soul is aching for the comfort and sustenance of the creator, be encouraged knowing that the "man after God's own heart" experienced the very same longing that you do. This hunger is what it means to be human, and it is what leads us to "praise," "bless," "meditate," and "sing," all of which we will talk about in the chapters to come.

APPLY TO LIFE

1. Take five minutes to think about how you got here and your spiritual path. Like David, maybe it has been a rough road, full of ups and down, yet through it all you still feel this tug — a desire for something more. If you are in a group, share your journeys with each other; if you are alone, write about your spiritual journey in a journal.
2. Building on the last exercise which had you look backwards, let us look forward now. Where do you want to be in your relationship with God? Do you want to feel his love? His presence? His forgiveness? Or maybe, you haven't experienced a personal God yet, and you want to start a relationship with Him. Do you feel that God will meet you where you are?

5

[Continue sharing answers to these questions or writing them down.]

3. Take out two sheets of paper. The first thing to do is write a letter to God. Express everything that you feel as honestly as you can. Like David in Psalm 42, let Him know how much you desire to be closer to Him. Explain your worries, your frustrations, your hopes, and your fears. Be vulnerable and talk about your longing for Him and your worries that this longing might not be reciprocated.

4. Next, you are going to write a letter from God to you. This is an imaginative exercise, and before writing, make sure that you pray for the Holy Spirit's guidance. As best as you can, try to listen to what God might be saying to you. Keep in mind the double longing we learned about and how God fervently chases after us, desiring a deep and intimate relationship.

FURTHER READINGS

Blackaby, Henry T., and Claude V. King. *Experiencing God: Knowing and Doing the Will of God*. B&H Publishing Group, 2004.

Calhoun, Adele Ahlberg. *Spiritual Disciplines Handbook: Practices That Transform Us*. InterVarsity Press, 2009.

Dybdahl, Jon L. *Hunger: Satisfying the Longing of Your Soul*. Energion Publications, 2015.

Foster, Richard J. *Celebration of Discipline: The Path To Spiritual Growth*. Harper Collins, 2009.

Willard, Dallas. *The Spirit of the Disciplines: Understanding How God Changes Lives*. Harper Collins, 2009.

CHAPTER 2

WORSHIP: GATEWAY TO COMMUNION

INVITE THE PRESENCE

Before you continue to dive deeper into God's word and discuss the One who is the receiver of your worship, it is important to first take the time to invite Him in. You can ask that He guides your worship and that it may be pleasing in His sight. Sing, read aloud, or thoughtfully ponder the following song.

I love you, Lord
~ Laurie Klein

Lyrics	Accompaniment	Listening

- https://genius.com/Laurie-klein-i-love-you-lord-lyrics (Lyrics)
- https://www.youtube.com/watch?v=c3xXkBVuQWU (Accompaniment)
- https://www.youtube.com/watch?v=V4uPwUrCaV0 (For Listening)

REVIEW THE READING

1. The first part of this chapter emphasizes the centrality of worship in our interaction with God (p. 13–17). Think about the most recent time you've been to church. What did worship

look like, and how important was it? How about in your daily life — what does worship look like, and how important is it to you?

2. Later, the chapter analyzed what worship is and what it isn't (p. 17–22). Look at the words for "worship" that are used in the Bible (p. 19 of *Hunger*) and think about what aspects of worship you are familiar with. Which of these words come to mind when you think of worship? Which of these words seem foreign and new to you when you think of worship?

3. The chapter ended with practical steps for understanding and experiencing worship (p. 23–24). See the application activities after the story for more specific guidance on this topic.

BIBLE STORY — EXODUS 15:1–21

Our next story comes from a time when God's chosen people, the Israelites, were in the process of escaping captivity in Egypt. At this point in time, the Israelites were enslaved by the Egyptians, who forced them into grueling labor, harvesting in the fields and creating bricks. The Israelites cried to God for deliverance, and God sent it through the man named Moses. Moses was an Israelite who had been raised as an Egyptian, though he had recently fled the country (the details of Moses' childhood and young adulthood can be found in Exodus 1–3). But God had heard the cries of the Israelites, and God decided that Moses would be the one that He would work through to bring about their deliverance. After some time, God sent Moses back to Egypt, where Moses contended with Pharaoh (the king of the Egyptians) regarding the enslaved status of the Israelites. God worked several incredible miracles through Moses which loosened Pharaoh's grip on the Israelites, allowing them to escape their bondage. Pharaoh gave pursuit, but God allowed His people to escape by parting the Red Sea and allowing His people to pass through unharmed. When Pharaoh and his chariots gave chase, the waves came crashing back down, ensuring the victory and freedom of the Israelites.

God had saved His people at last! After generations of persecution, belittlement and toil, the Israelites were finally free from their chains of enslavement. It is in this moment, after having crossed the sea and reaching dry ground on the other side, when Moses breaks into exuberant song:

> *Then Moses and the people of Israel sang this song to the Lord, saying, "I will sing to the Lord, for he has triumphed gloriously; the horse and his rider he has thrown into the sea. The Lord is my strength and my song, and he has become my salvation; this is my God, and I will praise him, my father's God, and I will exalt him," (Exodus 15:1–2).*

Notice that the text says that the people of Israel joined Moses in singing this song. Imagine how surreal this event must have been — thousands of people, all of their voices joined together in one song. The sound would have been tremendous! This amazing worship service didn't stop there — Moses' sister, Miriam, grabbed a timbrel and told the rest of the women to follow her. A timbrel was a musical instrument that resembles the modern tambourine. Along with all of the Israelite women, Miriam proceeded to break out into singing and dancing:

> *Sing to the LORD, for he has triumphed gloriously; the horse and his rider he has thrown into the sea.* (Exodus 15:21).

Now that would have been a sight! The Israelites had just finished walking across the floor of the red sea. Their feet were inevitably dirty and their clothes damp from the surrounding waters and mist. They were most likely sweaty from the beating of the sun and exhausted from their long journey. But that didn't stop them! I can only imagine what a sight it must have been, to behold all of these people jumping to and fro, elated because of their recent liberation.

APPLY TO LIFE

1. Close your eyes and imagine that you are one of the Israelites there on that day of God's deliverance. What would that have felt like? What would that make you want to do? Would you have burst out into song and dance, or would you have wanted to clean yourself first? After using your imagination, discuss your answers to these questions with your group or reflect on them by yourself.

2. The beautiful thing about worship is that it takes a variety of forms. It is all too easy for us to fall into what is comfortable and recognizable, and this can sometimes lead to a stagnation of our worship life. During your next devotional time with God, take some time to intentionally try a new way of worship

3. If you have not raised your hands before, try bringing your hands up as a symbolic way of receiving God's grace.

4. Engage in a physical expression to music, like dancing to a praise song or even doing something as simple as tapping the beat with your foot. These are all Biblical ways of worshiping God and help us better express our gratitude to Him for what He has done.

5. During your next worship time, try bowing before God and allowing your heart to mirror your body's posture of submission (see *Hunger* p. 19–24 for more ideas).

6. In the story of Moses and Miriam, God's deliverance is what drove them to worship Him. All too often, worship is relegated to just 20 minutes, once a week, during a church service. But some of the most authentic and beautiful worship seems to erupt spontaneously out of a recognition of who God is and what He has done for us. During this next week, try to intentionally take time out of each day to praise God for what He has done and what He is doing. This can be as simple as saying "Thank you so much Lord" after noticing a beautiful flower or singing the chorus of your favorite praise song while driving in your car.

FURTHER READINGS

Hayford, Jack Williams Jr. *Worship His Majesty*. Word (UK), 1987.

Neese, Zach. *How To Worship a King: Prepare Your Heart. Prepare Your World. Prepare The Way*. Charisma Media, 2015.

Redman, Matt. *The Unquenchable Worshipper: Coming Back to the Heart of Worship*. Gospel Light Publications, 2001.

CHAPTER 3

REPENTANCE, CONFESSION, AND FORGIVENESS

INVITE THE PRESENCE

Before you look at the word of a God who forgives you while you are still a sinner, it is important to first take the time to invite Him in. You can confess your sinful nature and repent of any wrongdoing, thanking Him for the forgiveness you have through Christ. Sing, read aloud, or thoughtfully ponder the following song.

> Out of the deep I call,
> To Thee, O Lord, to Thee,
> Before Thy throne of grace I fall;
> Be merciful to me.
>
> Out of the deep I cry,
> The woeful deep of sin,
> Of evil done in days gone by,
> Of evil now within.
>
> Out of the deep of fear
> And dread of coming shame;
> All night till morning watch is near
> I plead the precious name.

> Lord, there is mercy now,
> As ever was, with Thee,
> Before Thy throne of grace I bow;
> Be merciful to me.

> ~ Henry Baker

REVIEW THE READING

1. The third chapter begins with a look at repentance in the Bible (p. 25–28). Look on page 27–28 at the difference between sins and **SIN** — what does it look like to confess our **SIN** and not just our sins? Might it be harder to confess our **SIN** because it is more humiliating for us to admit to, or maybe confession is hard because we have difficulty noticing **SIN** due to its ingrained nature?

2. After looking at repentance, we turn to the topic of confession and how important honesty is in the process of confessing (p. 29–30). When confessing, why is it important to always be honest?

3. We then turn to forgiveness and learn its significance in the context of the Bible and our lives as Christians (p. 30–33). On page 31 we learn that forgiveness does not mean forgetting, condoning, pardoning, or necessarily leading to reconciliation. Why do you think that it is important to maintain these qualifications?

4. Lastly, we listened to practical advice on how to employ repentance, confession and forgiveness in our daily lives (p. 33–36). See the application section after the Bible story for some specific activities you can participate in.

BIBLE STORY — 2 SAMUEL 11–12

David had been King for a while and was engaged in a war that was going quite well for him. His army had just defeated the Syrians and was currently engaged in a conflict with the Ammonites. If you recall, David's ascension to the throne was not without difficulty, and at this point David had to have been feeling good about all that he had accomplished. So good that instead of going out to battle, he sent his general in his place. While lounging at the palace one day, David looked out over the tall roof of his palace and saw a woman bathing on the roof of one of the houses below. David inquired as to who she was and discovered that she was Bathsheba, wife of Uriah the Hittite (who was off at the battle). Overcome with lust, David ordered that she be brought to him, and he slept with her. Soon after, Bathsheba realized that she had conceived, and she sent news to David.

The next day, David ordered that Uriah return from the battle, hoping that Uriah would sleep with his wife. But like the good soldier he was, Uriah refused to go to his wife's chambers while his brothers in arms were still fighting on the battlefield. Exasperated with his unsuccessful attempt at covering up his sin, David sent orders to his general to put Uriah at the front of the battle lines and then to draw away from him in the heat of battle so that he might be killed. After Uriah died in the ensuing battle, David married Bathsheba and she bore him a son.

After a visit from the prophet Nathan, David realized his fault. And in his first act of repentance and confession, David acknowledges: "I have sinned against the Lord." (2 Samuel 12:13). In the truest form of repentance, David does nothing more than acknowledge his sin and repent. There is honesty in his confession — David makes no excuses, he doesn't try to lessen his sins, and he doesn't try to blame it on someone else. The second part of the very same verse shows us how quickly God moves to forgive: "David said to Nathan, 'I have sinned against the Lord.' And Nathan said to David, 'The Lord also has put away your sin; you shall not die,'" (2 Samuel 12:13). Even after rape and murder, it takes God no longer than one verse to forgive David. After the simplest act of repentance, God has already moved toward forgiveness. This does not mean that David does not have to deal with the consequences of his actions; David's son dies, and violence plagues his family for the remaining years of his life. These consequences may seem unfair to us because our concept of guilt is usually independent, whereas in that society, if you are guilty, other parts of your family were considered guilty as well and included in the punishment. Even though our culture understands sin and guilt differently, this story still shows us that our God is a God who is quick to forgive, while also not withholding the necessary consequences.

APPLY TO LIFE

1. Think about a moment in your life where you did something that you are ashamed of. Like David, maybe you have pushed what you did to the side because thinking about it was too painful. When you think about your situation in the context of your relationship with God, do you feel like you have to make excuses when you are confessing to God? If you do, what does this say about your perception of God? What does it look like to trust in God's forgiveness? Discuss these questions with your group or reflect on them by yourself.

2. On page 35 of *Hunger*, we talk about the importance of finding a small group or person whom with we can have honest, intimate talks about our life and spiritual difficulties. We challenge you to find such a group or person, and once trust is built, to open up about your "secret sins". Often, like David, we have sins that we are too ashamed to admit out loud until someone else speaks up and keeps us accountable for our actions. For David, it was the prophet Nathan that kept him accountable. Once you find a group/person (as outlined on p. 35 of *Hunger*), we challenge you to take the first step of confessing and asking for accountability.

3. Get a piece of paper and draw a line through the middle of it, creating two columns. Label one column "sin" and the other column "**SIN**" (*Hunger* p. 27–28). Looking at this story, what

were David's sins (write this down in one column)? What was his **SIN** (write this down in the other column)? Was his **SIN** lust, or was it something deeper? You can repeat this practice for yourself and analyze your own life as well.

FURTHER READINGS

McCullough, Michael E., Steven J. Sandage, and Everett L. Worthington Jr. *To Forgive Is Human: How to Put Your Past in the Past*. InterVarsity Press, 1997.

Miller, J. Keith. *A Hunger for Healing: The Twelve Steps as a Classic Model for Christian Spiritual Growth*. Harper Collins, 2011.

Seamands, David A. *Healing of Memories*. David C Cook, 1985.

CHAPTER 4

PRAYER AND MEDITATION I

INVITE THE PRESENCE

You are going to encounter the word of the one you pray to, but it is important to first take the time to invite Him in. You can ask Him to open your heart and to guide your prayers so that you may draw ever closer to Him. Sing, read aloud, or thoughtfully ponder the following song.

Accompaniment	Listening

- https://www.hymnal.net/en/hymn/h/445 (Accompaniment)
- https://www.youtube.com/watch?v=Gf11rReeWIs (For Listening)

Take my life, and let it be
Consecrated, Lord, to Thee;
Take my moments and my days,
Let them flow in ceaseless praise,

19

Take my hands, and let them move
At the impulse of Thy love;
Take my feet and let them be
Swift and beautiful for Thee,

Take my will, and make it Thine;
It shall be no longer mine.
Take my heart; it is Thine own;
It shall be Thy royal throne,

Take my love; my Lord, I pour
At Thy feet its treasure–store.
Take myself, and I will be
Ever, only, all for Thee,
Ever, only, all for Thee.

~ Francis Havergal

REVIEW THE READING

1. This chapter in *Hunger* focuses on prayer, beginning with an exploration of prayer in the Bible and how we ought to define it (p. 38–40). Think about prayer in your own life — what do your prayers sound like? What does your prayer life say about the values and assumptions you have related to prayer and God?

2. Using prayer in the Bible as a starting point, we then delve into the task of defining what prayer is and what it isn't. On page 40, I suggest that prayer is "reaching out to share with God as Friend and Lord," which highlights both the intimate aspect of our relationship with God (as Friend) and the submissive aspect of our relationship with God (as Lord). How would we be missing out on fully experiencing authentic prayer if we

only highlight one aspect of our relationship with God and neglect the other?

3. The chapter concludes by talking about how to pray, and we read seven suggestions that open more windows on prayer (p. 43–49). What might you have never considered as being a prayerful activity? What do you think about this wider definition of prayer?

BIBLE STORY — MARK 1

Jesus was a very busy man. The gospels are filled with details regarding the many different places that He traveled to, preaching to and healing the people who came to see Him. At the beginning of Mark's Gospel, we get a glimpse into one full day of Jesus' busy life. In the morning, Jesus was walking alongside the Sea of Galilee when He saw two brothers, Simon and Andrew. Jesus said to them "Follow me, and I will make you become fishers of men." (Mark 1:17). Immediately, they dropped their fishing nets and joined Him on His journey. Soon after, brothers James and John left their boats and joined Jesus and His other two disciples on their walk. Once they reached Capernaum, Jesus entered the synagogue and began teaching, for it was the Sabbath. The people in attendance were astonished at Jesus' teaching, as He taught as one who had authority. All of the sudden, a man with an unclean spirit cried out in the synagogue! Jesus rebuked the demon and commanded it to come out. The unclean spirit left the man, and the crowd was amazed.

Jesus then left the synagogue and went to the house of Simon and Andrew. Simon's mother-in-law was sick, and Simon was very concerned about her. Jesus came to her, took her by the hand, and healed her. At sundown, many more sick and possessed people were brought to Jesus at the house of Simon and Andrew, and Jesus proceeded to heal many and cast out the demons that plagued them. And finally, His day was over, and He went to bed.

The detail that is most pertinent to this lesson is what comes next — Mark tells us what Jesus does after his incredibly busy day:

"And rising very early in the morning, while it was still dark, he departed and went out to a desolate place, and there he prayed" (Mark 1:35). After such an exhausting day, the first thing on Jesus' mind was prayer. For Jesus, prayer was a refuge and retreat. His communication with the Father was an absolutely necessary part of His ministry, so much so that we see Jesus waking up early to ensure that He would have His time alone with the Father. Jesus didn't just *find* time for prayer, He *made* time for prayer. This is a pattern that we observe throughout all four Gospels — Jesus consistently engaging in prayer throughout all phases of his ministry.

If prayer was so important for Jesus, shouldn't it be just as important for us? After all, as Christians, we believe that Jesus and the Father were one since the beginning of time. If communion with the Father through prayer was important for Jesus, the man who knows Him better than any other, then it is nothing less than essential for us. Our lives do get busy, and the cares of this world are constantly begging for our attention. But when we look at one day in Jesus' ministry in Mark 1, we can take comfort in the fact that Jesus knows what it is like to be busy. He knows what it is like to have a day that seems like it just doesn't have enough hours, which is why He shows us that prayer ought to be a priority in our lives so that God might sustain us and give us strength.

APPLY TO LIFE

1. Are you a busy person? Look at your schedule for the coming week and pick the day that seems to be the most busy/stressful for you. Plan right now to set aside a part of that day for solitary prayer. Prayer was rejuvenating for Jesus, why does it not always feel that way for us? Share the method you picked and why, or write it down to keep yourself accountable.

2. As I talk about on page 40 of *Hunger*, it is crucial to see God both as friend and as Lord. Begin a prayer to God (as you normally would), and either write down what you say or pay close attention to your words and attitude. Do you tend to

emphasize your "friendship" with God, maybe to the detriment of His Lordship? Or do you tend to emphasize the "Lordship" of God, maybe to the detriment of your friendship with Him? Take some time for introspection and self-analysis.

3.   For this activity, we would like you to look at all of the different methods of prayer that are listed in *Hunger* on p. 43–48. Pick one of these pathways to prayer that you have not experienced yet, and try it out, asking God to lead you as you pursue Him. Share the method you picked and why, or write it down to keep yourself accountable.

FURTHER READINGS

Duewel, Wesley L. *Mighty Prevailing Prayer.* Zondervan, 1990.

Foster, Richard. *Prayer: Finding the Heart's True Home.* Hodder & Stoughton, 2008.

Keller, Timothy. *Prayer: Experiencing Awe and Intimacy with God.* Penguin, 2014.

Chapter 5

Prayer and Meditation II

Invite the Presence

Before approaching the word of the one whom your heart chases after, it is important to take the time to invite Him in. You can ask Him to settle your thoughts and feelings so that your meditations will draw you closer to Him. Sing, read aloud, or thoughtfully ponder the following song.

Accompaniment	Listening

- https://www.youtube.com/watch?v=3bQF3icqqEU (Accompaniment)
- https://www.youtube.com/watch?v=_2eSfKqMRbA (For Listening)

I come to the garden alone,
While the dew is still on the roses;
And the voice I hear, falling on my ear,
The Son of God discloses.

And He walks with me, and He talks with me,
And He tells me I am His own,
And the joy we share as we tarry there,
None other has ever known.

He speaks, and the sound of His voice
Is so sweet the birds hush their singing;
And the melody that He gave to me
Within my heart is ringing.

I'd stay in the garden with Him
Tho' the night around me be falling;
But He bids me go; thro' the voice of woe,
His voice to me is calling.

~ Austin Miles

REVIEW THE READING

1. This chapter begins by discussing the different instances of meditation in the Old and New Testament (p. 51–56). Why do you think that some aspects of Biblical meditation are under-emphasized or pass by unnoticed?
2. Using Biblical meditation as a cornerstone, a working definition of "meditation" is produced, while highlighting the differences between Christian meditation and other forms of the practice (p. 56–59). Why do you think it is important to keep the Bible central while meditating? How do you think your practice of prayer can relate to your practice of meditation?
3. This chapter ends with guidelines for implementing meditation into one's own spiritual life (p. 59–63). How do you think this form of Christian meditation can be beneficial for your spiritual life? How important do you think meditation is for professing Christians?

BIBLE STORY — MATTHEW 4:1-11

At the beginning of the Gospel of Matthew we learn about Jesus' birth and baptism. Before all of the stories of miracles, signs, and message, Mathew wants to show us the preparation that went into Jesus' ministry. At the very tail end of this "preparation stage" before beginning His ministry, Jesus was led into the wilderness. You might think that this was to be the "calm before the storm" and a time for him to relax before the busy years ahead, but that was not the case. Once in the wilderness, Jesus was tempted by the devil three times.

When the devil first came to tempt Jesus, he targeted Jesus' physical desire, challenging Him to turn the stones to bread. Jesus replied with a quotation from the Hebrew scriptures, rebuking the devil and refusing the temptation of sustenance. After this attack fails, the devil takes Jesus to the very top of the temple of the holy city (Jerusalem), challenging Jesus to throw Himself down and prove that he is the son of God by surviving. What is interesting about this temptation is that the devil actually quotes scripture to prove his point. But Jesus knew that this was a twisting of the true scriptural meaning and retorts with another passage, rebuking the devil for putting God to the test. For the last temptation, the devil upped the ante and showed Jesus all of the kingdoms from all across the world, saying that they would be placed under Jesus' authority if Jesus would only bow to him. Jesus replies with one last scripture, saying that we should worship and serve God alone. After this, the temptation was finished, and Jesus was cared for by the angels.

It is not a stretch to say that these 40 days were the hardest of Jesus' life. The physical toll of fasting, the mental toll of isolation, and the spiritual toll of temptation must have been brutal. But there is an important message located within this story that we might look over at first glance. In response to each of the devil's temptations, what does Jesus do? Each time, He quotes scripture. It is highly unlikely that Jesus brought a scroll out into the desert with him, which means that He knew these scriptures by heart.

Jesus was meditating on the scriptures during His 40 days in the desert, which is why they were in the front of His mind and on the tip of His tongue when the devil came to tempt Him.

Though some may look down on meditation because they associate it solely with eastern religion, we discover here that meditation is actually a Biblical principal. During the most important phase of His preparation for ministry, Jesus spent His time meditating on the word of God, in quietness and isolation from others. His meditation was guided by the Holy Scriptures, which enabled Him to see through the devil's lies and deceptions when the time of temptation came. If Jesus spent 40 days meditating and ruminating on the word of God, how much more ought we to take a few minutes out of our day to do the same?

APPLY TO LIFE

1. Have you practiced Christian meditation before? In the book *Hunger* on pages 60–61, you will read a step-by-step process on how to begin the process of one form of Christian meditation. If you are in a group, we encourage you to take a few minutes and practice this exercise as a group. After you are finished with your meditations, take time to share and discuss the experiences that you have had. If you are alone, follow the meditation guidelines and then write about your experiences in a spiritual journal.

2. When the devil tempted Jesus, Jesus rebuked him with specific Bible verses that dispelled the devil's lies and deception. What is something that the devil has tempted you with recently, or what is a lie that he has been telling you? Once you identify this point of attack, search the scriptures for a Biblical passage of truth that refutes the devil and his temptation. Spend several minutes repeating this scripture passage to yourself until you have memorized it. The hope is that whenever the devil tempts you again throughout your week, you would remember the

scripture that you have been meditating on and that you use it to rebuke the devil.

3. When Jesus went into the desert, it was quiet and isolated. Nowadays, with our computers, TVs, and smartphones, we have distractions waiting for us at every turn. Silence is an integral aspect of Christian meditation, and it is essential if we are trying to listen to the message that God may be trying to give us. Turn your phone off and take five minutes to just sit in silence. Then discuss or reflect about how this silence felt, whether it felt spiritual, refreshing, awkward, ordinary, etc. There are many different types of Christian meditation, focusing on spiritual elements such as silence, scripture, and visualization that are expanded upon in the further readings below (such as *The Joy of Listening to God*).

FURTHER READINGS

Huggett, Joyce. *The Joy of Listening to God: Hearing the Many Ways God Speaks to Us*. 1986 edition. IVP Books, 1987.

Kaplan, Aryeh. *Jewish Meditation: A Practical Guide*. Schocken Books, 1985.

Morgan, Robert. *Reclaiming the Lost Art of Biblical Meditation: Find True Peace in Jesus*. Thomas Nelson, 2017.

CHAPTER 6

STUDY AND GUIDANCE

INVITE THE PRESENCE

Before you open the word of God to study it, it is important to first take the time to invite Him in. You can ask Him to give you an open heart to receive whatever guidance He might have for you. Sing, read aloud, or thoughtfully ponder the following song.

Word of God Speak

~ Pete Kipley (MercyMe)

Lyrics	Accompaniment	Listening

- https://www.lyrics.com/lyric/6275444/MercyMe/Word+of+God+Speak (Lyrics)
- https://www.youtube.com/watch?v=S4o5auZfRsE (Accompaniment)
- https://www.youtube.com/watch?v=4JK_6osCH74 (For Listening)

REVIEW THE READING

1. The chapter begins by talking about how *true study* means listening to God. You will see the five steps that come with

     true study — repetition, concentration/focused listening, comprehension, reflection and reliving, and holy purpose (p. 65–68). Why do you think this level of intentionality is important when it comes to studying God's word?

2.   After talking about *true study*, the next topic is God's guidance. The chapter first addresses how to discern God's guidance (p. 68–70). Why do you think it is important to avoid the two extremes talked about on page 68 (never seeing God's guidance versus seeing it in every specific instance)?

3.   Then, you will read about the many different ways that God guides us (p. 70–75). In which of these ways does it seem like God speaks to you the most? In which of these ways have you maybe not given God a chance to speak?

4.   The chapter ends with a section on learning how to test God's guidance (p. 75–77). Do you think that it is possible to be 100% certain that specific guidance is from God?

BIBLE STORY — LUKE 24:13–35

Can you imagine how discouraged many of Jesus' disciples must have been after he died? The man that they had followed for years, the one who had taught and healed them, the one who many hoped would overthrow Rome and save them, was dead. If Jesus was the Messiah that was promised, then what were they supposed to do now that he wasn't there to lead them?

It is in this precarious position that we encounter two followers of Jesus traveling from Jerusalem to Emmaus. They were talking about everything that had just happened — how Jesus overturned the money tables, how He had been put on trial, and how He had been crucified. When a strange man approached them, they explained all of these things to Him. They also mentioned how some of the women found Jesus' tomb empty, but that when they went to look for themselves, they didn't encounter Jesus. The Bible tells us that while these two believers were recounting their experiences to the stranger, they "stood still, looking sad" (Luke 24:17, ESV).

As the reader, we know that the stranger they are speaking to is Jesus, but they were not able to recognize Him in this moment. Jesus meets their discouragement with admonishment and turns with them to the Holy Scriptures.

Jesus walked through the Scriptures with these two believers, showing them all of the signs that pointed to Him from beginning to end. We are told that Jesus began with Moses and all the Prophets but continued on to show them how all of the scriptures spoke about him. These two men, astonished with the wise teaching of this stranger, begged Jesus to stay with them after their travels and to spend the evening with them in a nearby village. At dinner, Jesus pronounced a blessing over the bread, breaking it and giving it to them in a manner similar to the last supper. It was at that moment that they realized that this stranger was Jesus himself, and Jesus immediately vanished before their very eyes. They said to each other: "Did not our hearts burn within us while he talked to us on the road, while he opened to us the Scriptures?" (Luke 24:32).

This story shows us just how important the true study of scripture is for receiving guidance from God. When these believers were discouraged, Jesus turned with them to the scriptures to both figuratively and literally "open their eyes". A lot of times, we might be just like these followers of Jesus — discouraged, lost, and afraid. And Jesus might be right there alongside us, we just may not know it! But by turning to the scriptures, and studying them from beginning to end, we begin to see the larger picture. We begin to hear God speak to us in ways that we might previously have thought to be impossible, and we are able to see how Jesus has been right by our side this whole time.

APPLY TO LIFE

1. *True Study* is the spiritual art of listening to God. For this activity, take a small portion of scripture that you have read recently or one that you are familiar with. Spend 10 minutes studying this scripture passage, focusing on the five steps

of *true study* — repetition, concentration/focused listening, comprehension, reflection and reliving, and holy purpose (it might help to have pages 67–68 from *Hunger* handy). After the 10 minutes, take some time to reflect and share with others regarding how God may have spoken to you during this time, or write it down in your journal.

2. Like the believers on the road to Emmaus, we may have barriers that hinder us from realizing God's voice in our lives. You read about several barriers to discerning God's guidance on pages 68–69. Take a few minutes to read these over and identify one of the barriers that seems strongest in your life. If you are in a group, share what this barrier in your life is, and talk about what God might be trying to say to you if this barrier were removed. If you are alone, do the same and write down your responses.

3. When it comes to listening to God's voice, it is important to be cautious and test any guidance that we receive. The believers on the road to Emmaus immediately went to Jerusalem to tell more of Jesus' followers about what they had seen (Luke 24:33–35). If you are in a group, I encourage you to commit to sharing God's leading in your life with each other. Ask each member of the group to share ways that they think they see God moving in their lives. Then pray over each other, asking God give discernment and wisdom as you all move forward. If you are alone, seek out a trusted spiritual advisor or pastor with whom you can share God's leading in your life, and commit to sharing with that person at some later time.

FURTHER READINGS

Mulholland, M. Robert, Jr. *Shaped by the Word: The Power of Scripture in Spiritual Formation*. The Upper Room, 1985.

Kugel, James L. *How to Read the Bible: A Guide to Scripture, Then and Now*. Free Press, 2008.

Wink, Walter. *Transforming Bible Study*. Abingdon, 1980.

Chapter 7

Community

Invite the Presence

Before you open the word of the God who calls us into communion with each other, it is important to first take the time to invite Him in. You can ask Him to give you a missional and empathetic heart so that the body of Christ might flourish. Sing, read aloud, or thoughtfully ponder the following song.

We are companions on the journey,
~ Carey Landry

Lyrics (PDF)	Accompaniment	Listening

- https://www.seasonsonline.ca/files/Companions on the Journey.pdf (Lyrics)
- https://www.youtube.com/watch?v=vF69vBkcdGg (Accompaniment)
- https://www.youtube.com/watch?v=vF69vBkcdGg (For Listening)

Review the Reading

1. This chapter begins by examining the Biblical and historical basis for Christian community (p. 79–82). You learn that

community is bearing each other's burdens and watching over each other in love with the aim of discipleship (p. 80). Why do you think it is significant Jesus chose 12 disciples to spend most of His time with?

2.   You will then read about how these values of community apply to us today (p. 82–83). What have your experiences been like with small groups? How can we prevent Christian community from looking too much like the culture around us?

3.   This chapter ends with a section showing how to put community into practice today (p. 83–86). Throughout this chapter you read a lot about how the Methodist tradition put these values into practice — what do you think are some characteristics of the Methodist small groups that stand out to you as important?

BIBLE STORY — ACTS 2:42-47

In Acts 2, the Holy Spirit comes upon the disciples, much to their bewilderment and amazement. Jesus had just ascended into Heaven, and the disciples were in a liminal stage of their lives; they had been encouraged by Jesus' resurrection, but now that He was gone, what should they do next? With the pouring out of the spirit, the disciples began to speak in different languages, and after Peter stood up and gave a passionate sermon, about three thousand people were baptized (Acts 2:41). God had amassed a large new following unto himself, but the story doesn't stop there.

Making the decision to accept the Gospel was just the first step in the lives of these three thousand believers. If they were to serve Christ for the rest of their lives, they would need to come together and form a community. We are fortunate that the author of Acts gives us a look into the lives of these new believers in Acts 2:42–47. These believers began by devoting themselves to the teaching of the apostles, coming together with the breaking of bread and prayers. As a result of this immediate orientation toward Christ as the center of their community, we are told that many wonders and signs began to be performed. All of the believers had everything in common, sharing all of their possessions and giving to those who had need. They attended the temple and worshiped together, eating dinner together in each other's homes every day with glad and generous hearts. They praised God, and the Bible tells us that all the people liked these disciples because of their generosity and kindness. As a result of this vibrant community, the Lord added to their number daily those who were being saved.

Can you imagine what it would have been like to be a part of this early church community? We are told that this community originated in Jerusalem, after the events of the Passover and Jesus' crucifixion and resurrection. At this time, the Romans were in control of Jerusalem, and there was a lot of discord amongst the Jews, as many disagreed with each other on how to deal with their Roman overlords. Emotions were high, and people were still waiting for a military messiah to bring back the former glory of the Jews and Jerusalem. Yet the community we read of here runs contrary to all of these expectations. Instead of being divided, these new believers became unified. Instead of hoarding their possessions in fear of the increasing taxes, they shared their possessions freely with one another. Instead of retreating to their own comfortable space, they reached out to the people around them.

This description in Acts 2 of the new believers gives us a great vision for what Christian community should look like today. The community engaged in many of the things that we have learned about so far in *Hunger* — prayer, worship, and the deep study of teachings. But most importantly, they did all of these things together in community.

APPLY TO LIFE

1. One of the hallmarks of the Christian community in Acts 2 was the breaking of bread together. While we live in a different time and context, eating a meal together is still a common way for people to get to know each other. For the believers, this was

a staple of their faith, as they did this every day (Acts 2:46). For this activity, think about a person or family that you do not know too well, or someone that you haven't talked to in a long time. Invite them to come and dine with you this week. If we want to be in community with others, the responsibility of reaching out should fall on our shoulders.

2. If you are using this study guide in a group, take a moment to think about the small community that you have gathered with you today (if you are alone, think of a Christian community that you are a part of). When you imagine the community in Acts 2, what similarities are there between that community and yours? What differences are there? How might you be able to strengthen the community that you have, using this community in Acts 2 as an example?

3. On page 84 of *Hunger*, you read that honesty, love, and accountability are three principles that should be a part of the central structure of community. In your group, designate one person to take notes. Then, go around the circle and have each person talk about what is important to them in community. Often, we enter community with different expectations, which can lead to conflict. It is essential to be open and honest about the community that you are trying to form so that you can all keep each other accountable. The early believers kept each other accountable in their giving, studying, and eating together. What do you want your community to look like, and what steps will you take to keep each other accountable? Talk with your group about these questions and consider writing them down as a community covenant that you all can refer to as time goes on.

FURTHER READINGS

Banks, Robert J. *Paul's Idea of Community: The Early House Churches in Their Historical Setting.* Eerdmans, 1980.

Bonhoeffer, Dietrich. *Life Together: The Classic Exploration of Christian Community.* Harper Collins, 1978.

Hellerman, Joseph H. *When the Church Was a Family: Recapturing Jesus' Vision for Authentic Christian Community.* B&H Publishing Group, 2009.

CHAPTER 8

FASTING

INVITE THE PRESENCE

God sustains us with His word, and now is the time to invite Him in. It is important to ask Him to give you a dedicated heart and a steadfast mind so that you might honor Him with your fasting. Sing, read aloud, or thoughtfully ponder the following song.

In fasting we approach thee here
~ Paul Anderson

Lyrics	Music	Accompaniment

- https://www.churchofjesuschrist.org/music/text/hymns/in-fasting-we-approach-thee?lang=eng (Lyrics)
- https://www.churchofjesuschrist.org/music/library/hymns/in-fasting-we-approach-thee?lang=eng (Music)
- https://www.youtube.com/watch?v=GkWOL-LUq2A (Accompaniment)

REVIEW THE READING

1. The chapter begins with a basic definition of fasting and then cites several Biblical examples of the practice (p. 87–89). Before reading this chapter, what were some of the conceptions that you had about fasting?
2. The chapter then goes into the various reasons for engaging in this spiritual practice (p. 89–91). If fasting is mentioned so many times in scripture and has so many benefits, why do you think it is so often disregarded in Western churches?
3. At the end of the chapter are several guidelines for fasting. Some of these guidelines are personal, while others are corporate. In what ways can fasting from other activities besides just eating be spiritually beneficial?

BIBLE STORY — MARK 9:14–29

In Mark 9 we are told of one of the most majestic and awe-inspiring events of Jesus' life that some of the disciples were able to witness — His transfiguration. Jesus took Peter, James, and John up onto a high mountain all by themselves, and then something spectacular happened. His clothes began to give off light and became an intense white color. And all of the sudden, Moses and Elijah appeared, talking to Jesus. God spoke from the clouds, and Jesus told them to talk about none of this until the Son of Man had been raised from the dead. For Peter, James and John, this must have been an incredible experience. They would have just witnessed God's supernatural power in an inexplicable way, and their faith and conviction of Jesus' messianic role had no doubt been strengthened. But after coming down from the mountain after this incredible experience, what is the first thing that Jesus and the select three disciples encountered? A complete debacle.

While they were on the mountaintop, the rest of Jesus' disciples had gotten into an argument with the scribes (who were among the religious leaders of the day). There was a large crowd gathered about them causing a ruckus. The disciples were being accused because they had failed to cast out an evil spirit from a boy that had been brought to them. The scribes were most likely using this failed exorcism as evidence of Jesus' misguided teachings, arguing that Jesus and the disciples were wrong in their attempts to cast out the spirit. In response to the drama, Jesus demonstrated his power and anointing by commanding the evil Spirit to come out of the boy, and the boy was healed.

The disciples were embarrassed. Jesus had gone away for a very short amount of time, yet they had already failed in His absence. Distraught, they pulled Jesus aside so they could talk to Him in private. "Why could we not cast it out?" they asked Him (Mark 9:28). And Jesus replied with an answer I am sure they did not expect: "This kind cannot be driven out by anything but prayer and fasting" (Mark 9:29).

Fasting was the key to casting out this difficult demon. While fasting may not be a spiritual practice that is given much attention today, it was of extreme importance for Jesus. In chapter five of this study guide we talked about how Jesus began His ministry by spending 40 days in the wilderness (Matthew 4), and it is important to note that He was also fasting from all food during that time. For Jesus, fasting was not only an integral part of His relationship with His Father, but it was also an integral part of His ministry of healing. Fasting was a spiritual discipline that Jesus expected his disciples to practice so that they might minister effectively. If we are going to take what Jesus says in this verse seriously, then we ought to heed Jesus' words and example on the importance of fasting. We are in a situation very similar to the disciples who weren't at the transfiguration, and Jesus is no longer physically manifested on this earth today. If we are ministering and spreading the Gospel, we are going to encounter many evil spiritual forces and demons in this world, and it is important for us to prepare for these conflicts by fasting.

APPLY TO LIFE

1.   As you may expect, the first activity this week is to engage in a fast. If you are in a group, I would encourage you to consider engaging in a corporate fast, as this may be a helpful way of introducing those who have never done it before to the practice. Take some time to talk about your reasons for fasting, what the fast will entail, and what you plan to do (or reflect on) during the time you would normally eat. Make sure that you reflect on your fasting experience together the next time you meet.

2.   The next activity takes the practice of fasting and applies it to your own individual context. Think about something that you do every day that feels like it is an integral part of your daily routine and talk about it in your group. For many of us, this will include things like watching TV, smartphone usage, or drinking coffee. While none of these things are inherently bad (just as food is not inherently bad), we stand to gain a lot when we give up the things that we "depend" upon so that we may reflect on the One that truly sustains us. During this upcoming week, engage in a fast from the activity that you have decided upon.

3.   In our Bible story today, as well as on page 93 of *Hunger*, you read that fasting is best combined with the other spiritual disciplines. As you are fasting throughout this next week (whether it is from food or something else), try to pay attention to your inner thoughts and feelings. Every time that you feel an urge for food (or the activity that you have given up), say a short prayer in your head, asking Him to be your sustenance and thanking Him for everything that He has done, is doing, and will do in your life. As time goes on, you will notice a shifting of your heart, as you grasp and feel on a deep level what it means to hunger after God. If you are alone, write down your answer to the same question- what is most important to you when you are in community with others?

FURTHER READINGS

Piper, John. *A Hunger for God*. IVP, 2013.

Towns, Elmer L. *The Beginner's Guide to Fasting*. Baker Books, 2010.

Wallis, Arthur. *God's Chosen Fast: A Spiritual and Practical Guide to Fasting*. CLC Publications, 2011.

CHAPTER 9

SOLITUDE AND SIMPLICITY

INVITE THE PRESENCE

Caught up in the business of life, we often have difficulty discerning God's word in our lives. It is important to pray and ask that He gives you the mindfulness that comes with solitary prayer and an uncluttered heart. Sing, read aloud, or thoughtfully ponder the following song.

In solitude
~ Ruth Duck

Lyrics (PDF)

- https://jamestownmeeting.org/wp-content/uploads/2020/05/In-Solitude-I-Come-to-God-in-Prayer.pdf (Lyrics)

REVIEW THE READING

1. The chapter begins by relating solitude to silence and retreat. You then read of the many benefits of such solitude (p. 95–97). Why do you think that so many people are afraid of being alone with God?

2. You then encounter several practical steps for practicing solitude (p. 98–99). Which of these examples resonates the most with you? Are these silent moments of listening for God the same as prayer?

3. After talking about solitude, we move on to defining simplicity and how it is very difficult to attain in Western culture today (p. 99–101). Why do you think the West has so often ignored the virtue of simplicity? Do you think this bias affects how we might read the Bible or perceive God in the world around us?

4. The chapter ends with several practical suggestions for simplicity, as well as some of the enemies that stand in our way (p. 102–103). Is getting rid of everything that holds us back from a life of simplicity the best way to go? Or does the answer lie in moderation?

BIBLE STORY — MARK 6

Jesus performed many miracles in His lifetime, but the largest miracle that He performed in front of the most people was undoubtedly the feeding of the five thousand. At the beginning of Mark 6, Jesus had sent out the twelve apostles to minister and cast out unclean spirits (Mark 6:7–13). This commission was itinerant in nature, as Jesus had advised the disciples to move from house to house, depending on how well their message was received. Indeed, when the disciples return to Jesus to give Him a report of their ministry, Mark tells us that they were so busy coming and going that "they had no leisure even to eat" (Mark 6:31, ESV). And while Jesus endorsed their ministry, He knew that something else was important also — solitude and rest.

Jesus tells the disciples to "come away by yourselves to a desolate place and rest a while," (Mark 6:31, ESV). Even though healing, proclaiming the coming of the kingdom, and driving out demons were of the utmost importance, Jesus showed the disciples that rest and solitude were essential aspects of the spiritual life. But similar to how it is today, solitude and silence are fleeting and hard to come by. Mark tells us that many people saw the disciples and Jesus trying to get away, so they followed them and ambushed them on the other side of the lake. One can only imagine the fatigue and frustration of the disciples, but Jesus responded with compassion and began to teach them many things. There was a large crowd there listening to Jesus, but because the location was so remote, there was no food! So Jesus performed His largest miracle yet, turning five loaves and two fishes into enough food for all of the people. Mark tells us that there were five thousand men that were fed that day, which means that the total number would have been much more with women and children included.

After performing this marvelous miracle, what does Jesus do? He once again pursues solitude and silence, sending His disciples away alone once again and he goes up onto a mountain to pray. It is incredibly significant that after performing the biggest miracle in front of the largest amount of people, Jesus returns to be by himself with God. While everyone was pursuing the disciples and Jesus, Jesus was pursuing solitude. He didn't pursue it to the extent that He turned people away, but He pursued it in a way that shows us how important His alone time with God was and how it was an integral part of His spiritual life.

Nowadays, we are similar to the disciples in that we are often too busy to eat, but it isn't usually because we are spreading the gospel like they did. From our jobs to our hobbies to the phones in our pockets, it seems like there are always things competing for our attention. It is in these moments that we must remember Jesus' reaction to one of the biggest moments of His ministry — He escaped to a solitary place to pray.

APPLY TO LIFE

1. In our hectic 21st century lives, we often spend our time tuning things out so that we can focus. Solitude is the opposite of this — it is placing yourself in an environment with so little stimuli that you can tune *in* to everything around you. Sometime

49

this week, try to venture to a quiet place where you can be truly alone. It could be a room in your house, a spot in a park nearby, or in a church after hours. Sit in silence for an extended period of time and attune your ears to God's voice and how He may be leading in your life. Take on a posture of listening, not speaking.

2. Just as Moses, Jesus, and many of the early church fathers fasted in the desert, so too might you have a special place of solitude to where you can escape. For me, it was the running track at a park nearby where I would walk after dark and gaze up at the millions of stars that would present themselves in the open sky. In your groups, talk about where this special place of solitude might be for you and why it is so special. If you do not have a special place of solitude, think about a place where you could continually go to be alone with God.

3. The enemy of simplicity is most often that concern from which we cannot escape. Whether it is possessions, debt, digital media, or something else, our lives are overrun with concerns other than the Kingdom of God. Identify and share with your group what one of these idols are in your life that are standing in the way of you living a more simple and peaceful life. In your groups, commit to "giving away" something in your life that is causing you anxiety and keeping you from living the simple life that God calls us to live.

FURTHER READINGS

Foster, Richard. *Freedom of Simplicity*. Zondervan, 2005.

Peck, M. Scott. *The Road Less Traveled: A New Psychology of Love, Traditional Values and Spiritual Growth*. Simon and Schuster, 1978.

Barton, Ruth. *Invitation to Solitude and Silence: Experiencing God's Transforming Presence*. IVP, 2010.

CHAPTER 10

WHY NO URGENCY?

INVITE THE PRESENCE

To persevere in the spiritual disciplines, it is important to ask God to sustain you with His word. You can request that He makes Himself known to you, and that the reality of His involvement in your life becomes visible and apparent. Sing, read aloud, or thoughtfully ponder the following song.

We have seen Christ is reality:
But it's not sufficient just to see:
He in our experience must be
Everything to us.
We in prayer behold Him face to face,
In the Word and meetings know His grace;
But in daily life, in every place,
What is He to us?
Hallelujah! By His light we see
Oh, how real, how full our Lord will be
If we'll only turn to Him at every time,
in every day,
Every thing, in every way and—
Be specific for reality!
And be done with generality!
If we'll just apply Him, we will see
He's everything to us.

~ Unknown

REVIEW THE READING

1. The beginning of the chapter defines what our worldview is and how it can affect our thoughts and behaviors (p. 105–107). The perception of time was used as an example of how one's worldview affects their values, beliefs, and behaviors. How do you think understanding your own worldview might help you relate to other people?
2. You then read how your worldview affects your religious life and the way that you view and interact with God (p. 107–113). Look at figure 2 on page 108. What box does your worldview generally emphasize/deemphasize? What box does the culture you are in generally emphasize/deemphasize?
3. Our worldview also affects how we act within our religious life and the spiritual disciplines we choose to practice (p. 113–115). What are some tangible ways that you can employ a Christian theistic worldview? How does the Christian theistic worldview affect the way that we evangelize?

BIBLE STORY — ACTS 16:16–24

I have heard many things nowadays blamed on our secularized culture and how supposedly most people are beginning to neglect God and go astray. Some claim that things used to be better "back in the day" when people believed in God and in the spiritual things in life. However, the Bible shows us that ignorance of God's power on the earth isn't unique to our time and place.

In Acts 16, we encounter Paul and Silas on their way to pray. While walking, they encountered a female slave who was possessed by a spirit. This spirit allowed the woman to predict the future, and her owners had realized this and had been capitalizing on her peculiar talent. She earned them a great deal of money with her fortune-telling, and when her slave-masters looked at her, they no doubt saw an unlimited potential of dollar signs. But this woman began to cry out as Paul and Silas walked by, proclaiming that

"These men are servants of the Most High God, who are telling you the way to be saved," (Acts 16:17, ESV). Paul and Silas were patient at first, but it eventually got to the point that Paul became extremely annoyed. He commanded the spirit to come out of the woman in the name of Jesus, and the spirit left her.

This woman had most likely been possessed by this spirit for her whole life, or at least long enough for her slave owners to capitalize on her affliction. And all it took was a simple command by Paul to free the woman in the name of Jesus! One would think that this would surprise all of the people of that town, who had undoubtedly seen this woman before and heard or experienced her fortune-telling for themselves. Telling a fortune is an incredible power, but even more so the power to cast out such a spirit at the mention of a name. Yet instead of incredulity and reverence, the people and the slave owners respond with hate. We are told that the owners were frustrated that their money-making scheme was ruined, and so the owners and the crowd seized Paul and Silas and beat them in the marketplace. After their beating, they got thrown into prison.

What does one's worldview have to be to respond to a miraculous healing with anger and vengeance? The slave owners and the crowd saw what was happening, but they were only focused on what was in front of them and did not take a step back to see the larger picture. The King of the world had come to save and liberate, to declare the hostages of the devil free, but instead of realizing the power of this religious message that Paul brought to them, all that they saw was lost profit. When it comes to recognizing God's power and actions in the world, the problem goes beyond "culture" — we have a problem with our hearts. We would rather see what we selfishly want to see rather than seeing things for what they actually are. Just like the slaveowners, our self-interest often blinds us to the supernatural ways that God is acting in the world.

APPLY TO LIFE

Take out a piece of paper and draw one upside-down triangle
with four section each, just like the one found on page 106 of
Hunger. For your triangle, start by writing the behaviors and
actions associated with your topic. Then write down your
beliefs from which your actions spring, as well as the values
that inform your beliefs. Finish by contemplating and
reflecting on your worldview, on which everything is built..
For each of these triangles, write down your worldview of the
topic, and then what values, beliefs, and actions spring up out
of that worldview. An example of the concept of time can be
found on page 107 of *Hunger*. Here is another example for
family:

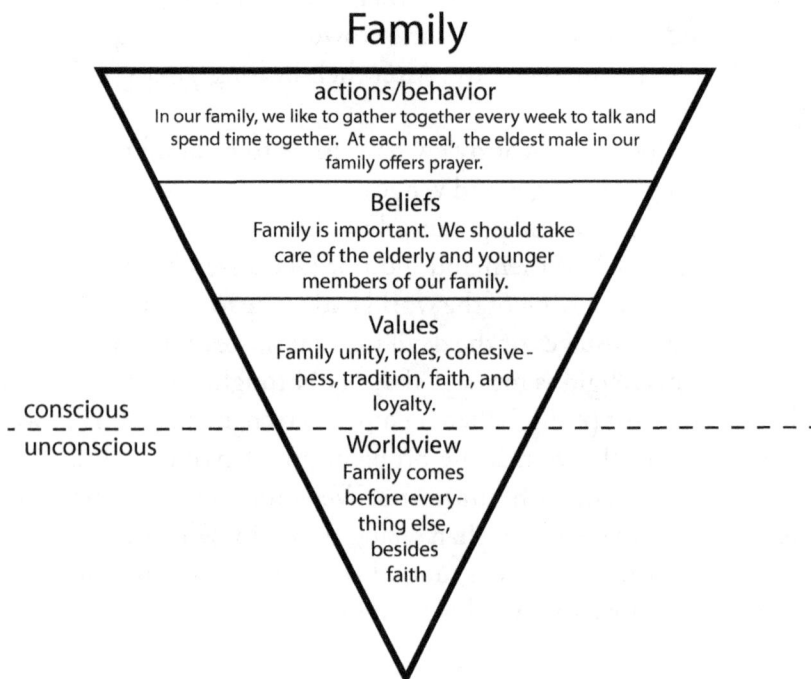

Family

actions/behavior
In our family, we like to gather together every week to talk and
spend time together. At each meal, the eldest male in our
family offers prayer.

Beliefs
Family is important. We should take
care of the elderly and younger
members of our family.

Values
Family unity, roles, cohesive-
ness, tradition, faith, and
loyalty.

conscious

- -

unconscious

Worldview
Family comes
before every-
thing else,
besides
faith

4. On page 108–109 we learn about the "excluded middle" of Western Culture and how people in those regions are often pressured to question the reality and validity of this middle level. A lot of the experiences that we have in this middle realm are kept quiet because we are afraid of being ridiculed or seeming crazy. However, within a group of believers, there ought to be no shame. In your group, take some time and share your experiences of this middle level with each other. If you are alone, write down these experiences and commit to sharing them with someone else. These can be experiences of angels, healings, spirits, or other unexplainable spiritual events. In sharing these happenings and talking about our experiences with them, we confirm their existence and better prepare ourselves to become aware of God and the devil's action in the world.

5. We can miss or gloss over God's action in our world simply because we are not looking for it. This next week, pay close and special attention to the way God might be acting in your life. This may be a dream with a prophetic meaning, a presence that you feel during your prayer time with God, or something else. Try employing the "Christian Theistic" worldview in an attempt to notice the places where the spiritual and physical realm are colliding. When something does happen, write it down and share it with those in your group next week. If you don't notice anything, that is ok! That is why it is important to share your experiences with the body of believers when you do have them, as it leads to mutual edification and a strong witness of God's action in the world.

FURTHER READINGS

Schwarz, Christian. *The Threefold Art of Experiencing God: The Liberating Power of a Trinitarian Faith*. ChurchSmart Resources, 1999.

Moreland, J.P. *Kingdom Triangle: Recover the Christian Mind, Renovate the Soul, Restore the Spirit's Power.* Zondervan, 2009.

Kelsey, Mortan. *Encounter with God: A Theology of Christian Experience.* Paulist Press, 1988.

CHAPTER 11

WHY IS MY EXPERIENCE DIFFERENT?

INVITE THE PRESENCE

Before you open the word of the God who makes each one of us unique, it is important to first invite Him in. You can ask Him to help you discern the personality traits and gifts that He has given you so that you might better serve Him. Sing, read aloud, or thoughtfully ponder the following song.

> Diff'rent gifts, yet we are one, one in Christ's body.
> ~ Maggie Russell[1]

Lyrics/Listen

- https://www.sixmaddens.org/different-gifts-aov-213/ (Lyrics/Listen)

REVIEW THE READING

1. This chapter starts by posing the question — why are we all so different (p. 117–118)? You then looked at the different personal temperaments through the Myers-Briggs model (p. 118–122). What do you think the limits of using this model might be when attempting to describe someone's personality?

---

1   Russell, Maggie. (1994). Different Gifts.

2. After looking at different personal temperaments, you turned to the myriad of different faith traditions (p. 123–124). Among the traditions discussed were the contemplative movement, the holiness tradition, the charismatic tradition, the social justice tradition, the evangelical tradition, and the incarnational tradition. Are there any other faith traditions or distinctions between faith traditions that you can think of? How about the sacramental/liturgical tradition (does it combine some of these types, or is it another category)?

3. The chapter concludes by discussing the unique cultural and psychological background you may have (p. 124–126). How might your own cultural and psychological background affect your relationship with God?

BIBLE STORY — JOHN 20–21

Different temperaments tend to become more pronounced and noticeable during times of importance and stress, and the people we learn about in the Bible are no exception. After Jesus' crucifixion, His disciples and followers were undoubtedly devastated. We are told that they "did not understand the Scripture, that he must rise from the dead," (John 20:9), so after His death they must have felt incredibly shocked and sad. They had just lost the one who they had thought was the Messiah. He was supposed to be the one to save them from Rome and to bring about the Kingdom of God, but how could he do all of that if He was dead? After Jesus is buried, we are told that the first person to the tomb was Mary Magdalene. She encountered the stone rolled away, and was initially shocked and excited, but upon discovering that the tomb was empty, she became dismayed (she probably thought that his body had been taken by the Roman guards or Pharisees). She began to weep outside of the tomb.

When Mary let the disciples know that the tomb was empty, Peter began to run toward the tomb. In his eagerness, he wanted to get to the tomb as fast as he possibly could to see what had happened to his teacher's body. One can only imagine how fast he ran! Upon arriving at the tomb, Peter saw the linen cloths lying in the tomb, but no body. He then "went away, wondering to himself what had happened." (Luke 24:12).

Jesus eventually appeared to Peter, and he rejoiced in his savior's resurrection, but there was one other disciple who was not so easily convinced. Upon hearing the news of the empty tomb and Jesus' appearance to the other disciples, Thomas did not believe that what they were saying could be true. He proclaimed that he simply could not believe unless he could put his finger into the nail marks and his hand on Jesus' side. Upon seeing Jesus eight days later, a surprised Thomas exclaimed: "My Lord and my God!" (John 20:28).

Not everyone reacted the same way to the disappearance of Jesus' body and his subsequent resurrection. Mary was sad because she thought his body was stolen. Peter was extremely excited and hopeful, but left the empty tomb perplexed. Thomas was doubtful and unconvinced, in need of validation by his own eyes. And yet, though all of Jesus' followers reacted in different ways with their own different temperaments, Jesus still appeared to all of them to comfort them and give them peace. Jesus meets us where we are, no matter what our personality traits are. Even though we may react differently to spiritual matters than our brothers and sisters in Christ, we can rest assured that we serve a God who loves people of all different temperaments.

APPLY TO LIFE

1.   Instead of just talking about the different Myers-Briggs personalities, why not figure out for yourself what yours is? For this activity, find a MBTI test online (a quick google search will show hundreds, many of them free) and take it. If you do not have access to a computer, talk with those in your group and try to decide which categories you fit in best. Once you know your personal temperament according to the MBTI

test, talk with those in your group about how this affects your spiritual life and interaction with others.

2. What faith tradition are you from? Take a few moments to map out your personal faith journey and note which tradition most closely relates to your past. If you are new to the faith, which of these traditions are you most in contact with? Once you have in mind the faith tradition you relate to most, share with your group or write down the many *positive* aspects this tradition brought about in your faith walk. Then, reflect on the more *negative* aspects this tradition has affected your journey. Talk about how this self-awareness of one's faith background might help one remain faithful in such a diverse and often divisive world.

3. This next activity will be more difficult for some. We have all experienced suffering and pain in our lives, and it inevitably affects our practice of the spiritual disciplines and our relationship with God. In your group, share with each other (as much as you are willing) a painful experience or relationship from your past that has deeply shaped you. After sharing your story, reflect out loud how this might affect the way that you see God or other people. If you are alone or not willing/able to share your story, writing down your experience and how it affects your relationship with God is fine.

FURTHER READINGS

Cron, Ian M, and Suzanne Stabile. *The Road Back to You: An Enneagram Journey to Self-Discovery*. IVP, 2016.

Keating, Charles J. *Who We Are Is How We Pray: Matching Personality and Spirituality*. Twenty-third Publications, 1987.

Keirsey, David, and Marilyn Bates. *Please Understand Me*. Prometheus Nemesis, 1984.

CHAPTER 12

ARE SPIRITUAL PRACTICES LEGALISTIC?

INVITE THE PRESENCE

God has revealed Himself through His son Jesus Christ to be a God of unimaginable grace. Before opening His word, it is important to invite Him in and ask Him to grant you perseverance as you chase after Him. Sing, read aloud, or thoughtfully ponder the following song.

Lyrics & Accompaniment

Listening

- https://www.hymnal.net/en/hymn/h/457
  (Lyrics and accompaniment)
- https://www.youtube.com/watch?v=SeSGLlYc7TQ
  (For Listening)

My life, my love, I give to Thee,
Thou Lamb of God who died for me;
O may I ever faithful be,
My Savior and my God!

I'll live for Him who died for me,
How happy then my life shall be!

I'll live for Him who died for me,
My Savior and my God!

I now believe Thou dost receive,
For Thou hast died that I might live;
And now henceforth I'll trust in Thee,
My Savior and my God!

O Thou who died on Calvary,
To save my soul and make me free;
I'll consecrate my life to Thee,
My Savior and my God!

~ Ralph E. Hudson[2]

REVIEW THE READING

1. This chapter begins by showing how the spiritual disciplines are not meant to be legalistic when they are understood in the light of God's grace (p. 127–129). Both justification and sanctification are gifts from God, and it is our job to "create space" for God to show up. Why do so many of us fall into the temptation of linking our salvation with our own works? How can the spiritual disciplines instead be a way of showing allegiance to God and thanking Him for who He is and what He has done?

2. The spiritual disciplines are then discussed within the metaphor of training (p. 129–132). One should strive to find the balance between structure and freedom. What are some examples of the spiritual disciplines being employed with too much freedom? What are some examples of the spiritual disciplines being employed with too much structure?

---

2   Hudson, Ralph. (1882). I'll Live for Him.

3. You are left with a Biblical mandate for sanctification and the spiritual disciplines (p. 132–134). The Bible shows us how God calls us to these practices and gives us the strength to carry them out. Do you think that God calls all believers to the same spiritual disciplines in the same proportion? Why or why not?

BIBLE STORY — MATTHEW 20:1-19

In Matthew 20 Jesus gives us a parable that shows why our relationships with God are not meant to be legalistic. Jesus says that the kingdom of heaven is like a landowner who went about searching for workers to work in his vineyard early in the morning. Upon finding a few, he agreed to pay them one denarius (back then, that was the normal daily wage for a laborer) for their labor and sent them to his field. Later in the morning, the landowner saw more workers lounging about in the marketplace and told them to go work in his field and that he would pay them whatever is right. And so, at nine in the morning, these workers went and joined the other workers that had gone into the field earlier. The landowner did the same thing at noon and at three, adding even more laborers to his growing total — he must have had a very big field! At five in the afternoon, he went out again, and he found a few more workers standing around. He asked them why they had been standing around all day, and the workers replied that they had been looking for work, but no one had hired them. The landowner once again told them to go and work in his vineyard, and they did.

When evening came and the workday was over, the landowner had his foreman call together all of the workers and he set about paying them. He began with the workers who were hired last (at five in the afternoon) and paid them one denarius. He called each worker forward in the reverse order that they had began working, and each received a denarius. When the workers who had been working in the vineyard since early in the morning came forward, they expected to be paid more than a denarius; after all, they had worked more than double the workers who had been hired in the afternoon! But no — each of these workers also received one denarius. They grumbled, complaining to the landowner that the pay wasn't fair when their coworkers had only worked one hour but they had worked all day. In reply, the landowner said—

> *I am not being unfair to you, friend. Didn't you agree to work for a denarius? Take your pay and go. I want to give the one who was hired last the same as I gave you. Don't I have the right to do what I want with my own money? Or are you envious because I am generous?* (Matthew 20:13–15, ESV).

When it comes to the spiritual disciplines, it can be easy to get discouraged when you feel like you aren't doing enough or that you have started too late. You might look to the side and see your brother or sister in Christ who has been working in the field all day, and when you compare yourself to them, wonder how it is possible that you might be saved. But that is the beauty of the kingdom of God — we are not saved by our acts. There is nothing we can do to earn God's gift, because He freely gives it to all of us, regardless of how long we have been working in the field. This kingdom of God is the opposite of legalism — it is grace.

APPLY TO LIFE

1. The path of the spiritual disciplines is a lifelong journey, and it can be helpful to set goals for yourself. Take out a piece of paper or your journal and write down three goals relating to the spiritual disciplines that you wish to reach within the next year. This could be developing a weekly pattern of fasting, establishing a consistent devotional time, or regularly using your prayer diary. Whatever your goal is, strive towards it knowing that you are free to do so within the grace given by God. In grace, commit to keeping those in your group accountable for their goals (for the importance of accountability, see chapter 7).

2. Because we want to meet God, it is important to make the space for Him. He does all of the work, but if there are things in our lives that are crowding our life, it will be difficult for us to notice and accept God when He does show up. Take five minutes and think about the elements of your life that are crowding you and preventing you from fully inviting God in. Share what you think of with your group and talk about ways to clear the clutter in your life.

3. For many, the spiritual disciplines have a long history of trauma because of the legalism that has been attached to them. As a group, turn in your Bibles to Romans 5:6–8. When Paul is writing these verses, he is writing them to the entire church, meaning they are just as true for us today as they were for Paul's community thousands of years ago. Have one person in the group close their eyes, and then read this blessing over them, inserting their name into the verse every time the verse says "we" or "us". E.g. "But God demonstrates His own love for Jon in this: While Jon was still a sinner, Christ died for Jon." Repeat this for every member of your group, experiencing the blessing of sanctification that Christ has given us free of charge.

FURTHER READINGS

Postema, Don. *Space for God: Study and Practice of Spirituality and Prayer*. Faith Alive Christian Resources, 1997.

Bounds, E.M. *Power Through Prayer*. Zondervan, 1961.

Whitney, Donald S. *Spiritual Disciplines for the Christian Life*. Nav-Press, 1991.

CHAPTER 13

WHAT ARE THE STAGES OF GROWTH?

INVITE THE PRESENCE

Before you open the word of the one who molds you and knows the number of hairs on your head, it is important to invite Him in. You can ask Him to empower you through His Holy Spirit to continue growing and developing in your spiritual journey. Sing, read aloud, or thoughtfully ponder the following song

There is a road meant for you to travel,
~ Michael John Poirier[3]

Lyrics (PDF)	Accompaniment	Listening

- https://www.seasonsonline.ca/files/Strength for the Journey.pdf. (Lyrics)
- https://www.youtube.com/watch?v=dYekrDnYKow (Accompaniment)
- https://www.youtube.com/watch?v=JhbXsoIScy8 (For Listening)

---

3   Poirier, Michael. (2004). Strength for the Journey. On *God is my Rock* *[CD]. World Library Publications.*

REVIEW THE READING

1. Spiritual growth is first defined and then related to other types of growth (p. 135–137). Just as we grow as children when we eat food, so too we grow in our faith when we commune with God. What are some ways spiritual growth is different from other types of growth?

2. Next you read about the four stages of spiritual growth as described by M. Scott Peck (p. 137–140). While these stages are not conclusive, they can give you a framework with which you can better understand your own spiritual growth. What do you think some of the shortcomings of this model might be?

3. You finish the chapter by reading about alternative ways of describing spiritual growth and how to continue along on your journey (p. 140–142). Why is it important to see the Christian race as more than just a "before conversion vs. after conversion" dichotomy?

BIBLE STORY — MARK

For the perfect example of spiritual growth, we don't have to look further than those who were closest to Jesus — His disciples. Jesus called twelve disciples to accompany Him during His ministry and to learn from Him so that they might be able to spread the good news when He was gone. Even though many renaissance paintings depict the disciples as old men with bald heads and grey beards, the reality of the situation couldn't be further from the truth. The disciples were most likely early teens between the ages of 12–20.[4] Thus, when Jesus calls them, it is no surprise that they show signs of the early stages of spiritual maturity. We can assume that the disciples were probably in stage two of Peck's four-stage spiritual maturity theory — the fact that they accepted Jesus' call and followed Him rules out the notion that any of them would be in stage one.

---

4   Cary, Otis, and Frank Cary. "How Old were Christ's Disciples?" *The Biblical World, vol. 50, no. 1, 1917, pp. 3–12.*

Stage two is characterized by structure and institution — characteristics we see often in the lives of the disciples. In Mark 10 James and John approach Jesus and ask Him to guarantee that they would sit at Jesus' right and left hand at the coming of His Kingdom. This seems like a reasonable request on the surface level, as almost all institutions function in the same way — those that support a King at an early stage of his rise are then elevated to positions of splendor once that King takes office. But Jesus scolds them, as His Kingdom is unique and doesn't adhere to the institutional "rules" of the world. In Jesus' kingdom, "whoever would be great among you must be your servant," (Mark 10:43).

Another example of the disciples in stage two is when Peter tells Jesus at the last supper that he will never disown or betray Jesus. For Peter, his allegiance to Jesus was black or white and he thought that he was sure of the future and what it would be. But in His wisdom, Jesus admonished the disciples, saying that "you will all fall away" (Mark 14:27). Stage three of spiritual growth is characterized by doubting convention and becoming skeptical. Jesus knew that all of the disciples had to question and doubt Him at some point in time, because only then would they be able to see the Kingdom of God for what it really was. The disciples might have previously thought that Jesus' ministry was about overthrowing Rome, but it was so much more than that. And when their world shattered after the crucifixion of Jesus, we can assume that they were plunged into a period of spiritual doubt, confusion, and skepticism. They had to doubt their own preconceptions about Jesus in order to understand the deeper meaning of His ministry and sacrifice.

To see the disciples progress from stage three to stage four we must look outside of Mark and toward Acts. Yes, in the Gospels the disciples do encounter Jesus once more, but their spiritual maturity is shown in Acts when they engage in ministry even when Jesus is not with them anymore. As Jesus has taught, "Blessed are those who have not seen and yet have believed," (John 20:29). Stage four is characterized by a connection to others and God as people embrace the mystery of His presence and being. The disciples show their spiritual maturity in their care for each other (like the church in Acts 2) and their peace and assurance through faith even in the face of persecution and death. The spiritual journey of the disciples continues to serve as a model for us today and encourages us to never become stagnant in our growth.

APPLY TO LIFE

1. It is easiest to see what direction you are headed in if you first know where you are. Have a conversation with those in your group (or reflect by yourself) about where you are in your spiritual journey in terms of Peck's four stages of spiritual growth. Are you a new believer, perhaps in stage two of spiritual growth? Or are you a more experienced believer in stage 4? Reflect out loud on your spiritual journey up until this point and how this determines what stage you are most likely in.

2. Last week you made three spiritual discipline goals for the next year. Think about these three goals and how they relate to you moving forward in your spiritual journey. Pull out your journal or the sheet of paper that you wrote your goals on, and now add how you hope these disciplines will affect your spiritual walk. For example, your goal could be: "To meditate twice a week on God's love and grace", and now you might realize that "This will help me grow from stage two of spiritual growth to stage three of spiritual growth as I become less legalistic and more focused on God's love rather than the actions of others". Share your reflections with those in your group.

FURTHER READINGS

Peck, M. Scott. *The Different Drum*. Simon and Schuster, 1987.

Peck, M. Scott. *Further Along the Road Less Traveled*. Simon and Schuster, 1988.

Groeschel, Benedict J. *Spiritual Passages: The Psychology of Spiritual Development*. Crossroad, 1986.

Chapter 14

What Should I Do Now?

Invite the Presence

As this book comes to an end, we ask that God continues to lead and guide us in the spiritual disciplines. It is important to ask that He gives us a listening heart for His word and the willingness to put what we hear into action. Sing, read aloud, or thoughtfully ponder the following song.

> Draw near to Jesus' table,
> Ye contrite souls, draw near;
> The hungry, sick, and feeble,
> His choicest dainties share.
> Let Jesus' death engraven
> Upon your hearts remain;
> Thus here, and there in heaven
> Eternal life you gain.
> They who hunger after Christ are fed;
> All the thirsty to life's fountain led;
> He the needy doth supply
> With good things abundantly,
> From his fulness they are nourished.
> Since he welcomes ev'ry soul distress'd,
> And hath promised to the weary rest,
> At his call we now draw nigh,
> He invites us graciously,
> Come, poor sinner, come, and share my feast
> -Unknown

REVIEW THE READING

1. The last chapter of this book begins by talking about the centrality and importance of the spiritual life, as well as the fruits that it brings about (p. 143–146). Religion that is based on doctrine or belief neglects the centrality of love and the heart in Jesus' ministry. What are some of the tangible fruits that you expect to see in your life as you grow in the spiritual disciplines?

2. The spiritual life extends into our relationship with others and our relationship with God (p. 146–147). It is important to be honest with God and acknowledge the central role of the Holy Spirit in your communion with God and others. What are some of the consequences of self-deception and arrogance when it comes to one's spiritual life?

3. The book ends by imploring you to not let your spiritual journey end here, but rather seek out other ways of growing (p. 147–150). Whether it be continued study, mentorships, or specific commitments, your spiritual growth should be a lifelong journey into which you invest continually. Why are submission and humility so important if you want to keep growing in your spirituality?

BIBLE STORY — MATTHEW 28

After Jesus' death, the disciples were confused and distraught. Wasn't he supposed to be the Messiah who came to save? How could He do that if He was dead? They thought that this was the end of their journey, but Jesus showed them that it was actually just the beginning. When the two Mary's went to Jesus' tomb, they found the stone rolled back with an angel sitting on it! The angels told them that Jesus had risen and that they were to tell the disciples to meet Him in Galilee. With joy, they hurried back, and suddenly ran into Jesus Himself! Jesus greeted them and repeated the angel's instruction to tell the disciples to meet him in Galilee.

When the disciples went up to the mountain where Jesus had told them to go, they saw Him there and worshiped Him. We are told that some also doubted. Then Jesus came to them and gave them what is known as the great commission:

> *All authority in heaven and on earth has been given to me. Therefore go and make disciples of all nations, baptizing them in the name of the Father and of the Son and of the Holy Spirit, and teaching them to obey everything I have commanded you. And surely, I am with you always, to the very end of the age* (Matthew 28:18–20).

At what seems like the end of the story, Jesus gave the disciples a new beginning. He gave them a call to go into the world and to make more disciples with the assurance that He would be with them always. As you are also disciples of Jesus, He gives you this call as well. This is not the end of your journey with the spiritual disciplines. Jesus calls you to go into the world and obey his teaching, spreading the good news of the Kingdom. And we are encouraged with the promise that He is with us as we do this, even to this day. The spiritual disciplines help us realize this fact so that it may propel us forward to witness by the power of the Holy Spirit. May we walk side by side on this journey until He comes again.

APPLY TO LIFE

1. If you do not already have a journal, I encourage you to create a "spiritual disciplines" journal. In it, write about your experiences with all of the spiritual disciplines and ways that you may feel God leading or speaking to you. If you already have one of these journals, share with your group how you plan to use it to continue in your journey of spiritual growth. If you do not have a spiritual disciplines journal, cconsider creating one.
2. One of the keys to continued spiritual growth is discipleship and mentorship (p. 148). We all should have at least one

spiritual mentor in our lives, and if we are spiritually experienced and mature enough, we should also have those that we are mentoring. Talk in your group about the mentoring relationships that you have and the mentoring relationships that you wish to create. Keep each other accountable for making mentorship an integral part of your spiritual journey.

3. The book *Hunger* is not the end of learning about the spiritual disciplines. The activities from each chapter have helped you practice the spiritual disciplines, but you should also continue educating yourself and learning more about them from fellow spiritual pilgrims. At the end of each chapter of this study guide there has been a "further reading" section. After finishing *Hunger*, I challenge you to pick up one of these other books and continue learning in the Spirit. Talk with your group about what book you plan to read next or what books might pique your interest.

FURTHER READINGS

Bacovcin, Helen, trans. *The Way of a Pilgrim: And the Pilgrim Continues His Way*. Image Books, 1978.

Kelly, Thomas R. *A Testament of Devotion*. HarperCollins, 1992.

Sanders, Oswald J. *Spiritual Maturity: Principles of Spiritual Growth for Every Believer*. Moody Press, 1994.

Development. Crossroad, 1986.

ALSO FROM ENERGION PUBLICATIONS

This study guide is based on

HUNGER

Satisfying the Longing of Your Soul

Jon L. Dybdahl

Second Edition

https://www.energiondirect.com/product/hunger